ENERGY FOR THE FUTURE

ENERGY FROM THE SUN

by Clara MacCarald

FOCUS READERS.

NAVIGATOR

WWW.FOCUSREADERS.COM

Focus Readers is distributed by North Star Editions:
sales@northstareditions.com | 888-417-0195

Produced for Focus Readers by Red Line Editorial.

Content Consultant: Timothy Smith, Professor of Sustainable Systems Management and International Business, University of Minnesota

Photographs ©: Shutterstock Images, cover, 1, 4–5, 7, 8–9, 15, 17, 20–21, 23, 25, 26–27, 29; Archive Farms Inc/Alamy, 10; Mark Williamson/Science Source, 12–13; MSFC/NASA, 19

Library of Congress Cataloging-in-Publication Data
Names: MacCarald, Clara, 1979- author.
Title: Energy from the sun / Clara MacCarald.
Description: Lake Elmo, MN : Focus Readers, 2022. | Series: Energy for the future | Includes
    index. | Audience: Grades 4-6
Identifiers: LCCN 2021032044 (print) | LCCN 2021032045 (ebook) | ISBN 9781637390597
    (hardcover) | ISBN 9781637391136 (paperback) | ISBN 9781637391679 (ebook) | ISBN
    9781637392164 (pdf)
Subjects: LCSH: Solar energy--Juvenile literature.
Classification: LCC TJ810.3 .M26 2022 (print) | LCC TJ810.3 (ebook) | DDC 621.47--dc23
LC record available at https://lccn.loc.gov/2021032044
LC ebook record available at https://lccn.loc.gov/2021032045

Printed in the United States of America
Mankato, MN
012022

ABOUT THE AUTHOR

Clara MacCarald is a freelance writer with a master's degree in ecology and natural resources. She lives with her family in an off-grid house nestled in the forests of central New York. When not parenting her daughter, she spends her time writing nonfiction books for kids.

TABLE OF CONTENTS

CHAPTER 1

SOLAR-ENERGY SOLUTION

In 2014, war broke out in Yemen. More than 100,000 people had died by 2021. People in Yemen struggled to meet their basic needs.

In 2019, ten Yemeni women wanted to help. The women decided to bring solar energy to their villages. Other community members thought women shouldn't work.

The war in Yemen devastated the country's electricity systems.

But this didn't stop the women. With help from the United Nations and the European Union, they set up a solar power plant.

The women mounted solar panels on strong frames. Every morning, they tended to the plant. They mopped the panels and checked for loose screws.

At first, the plant powered 25 homes. The women made money from selling electricity. They bought more **batteries**. With batteries, they could store the power until people needed it. The number of homes powered by the plant increased to 43. Villagers could run refrigerators, fans, and washing machines.

Solar panels have helped bring electricity to people in war-torn Yemen.

One electricity user bought a sewing machine. She started selling clothes to help support her family. Other villagers borrowed money from the group. They used the money to open more businesses.

Solar power can change the world. But energy from the sun can also change people's lives.

CHAPTER 2

SUN POWER

Solar energy is not a recent discovery. Ancient people used sunlight to heat south-facing buildings. They also started fires by directing sunbeams with mirrors.

In 1839, a French scientist made a new discovery. Certain **materials** give off electric charges when hit by light. The light causes chemical processes to

South-facing windows at a Roman bathhouse allowed sunlight to heat the baths.

Alexandre-Edmond Becquerel discovered the photovoltaic effect. It says that light can be used to create electricity.

happen in the materials. Those processes produce an electric current. People can use that current as electricity.

In 1954, American scientists made more progress. They produced the first workable solar cells. These devices turn sunlight into electricity.

Early solar cells were weak. They harnessed only 6 percent of the solar energy hitting them. But solar **technology** has improved over time. By 2020, solar cells could harness nearly 50 percent of solar energy. They have become a key alternative to **fossil fuels**.

PRESIDENTIAL PERSPECTIVES

US presidents have had different opinions on solar power. Jimmy Carter put solar panels on the White House in 1979. The next president was Ronald Reagan. He saw no future for solar power. He took the panels down. In 2002, George W. Bush added solar panels to the White House grounds. Barack Obama put panels back on the White House itself in 2013.

CHAPTER 3

SOLAR TECHNOLOGIES

Solar technologies make usable energy from sunlight. Some kinds make electricity. Others make heat. Either way, solar power is clean. It does not give off **greenhouse gases**. And the power is **renewable**. Solar cells work anywhere the sun shines. Every day, more sunlight shines on Earth.

Solar cells can even work in space. In 1958, the first orbiter with solar panels lifted off.

Solar cells are one kind of solar technology. Several solar cells make up a solar panel. A group of solar panels form a solar array. All of these convert sunlight into electricity.

Another solar technology is called **concentrating** solar power (CSP). A CSP plant also makes electricity. But first, it makes heat.

The plant has many mirrors. The mirrors reflect light from a large area onto a small area. The strong light heats up a liquid. It creates steam. The steam turns a wheel that powers a generator. This machine turns the energy of motion into electricity.

HOW SOLAR CELLS PRODUCE ELECTRICITY

Sunlight hits the top of a solar cell. The light energizes electrons in the cell, allowing them to move among the cell's layers. Electrons are negatively charged particles. So, they are drawn to the positive charge of one of the layers. They flow toward that layer. Metal strips collect the electrons and send them down a wire to be used or stored.

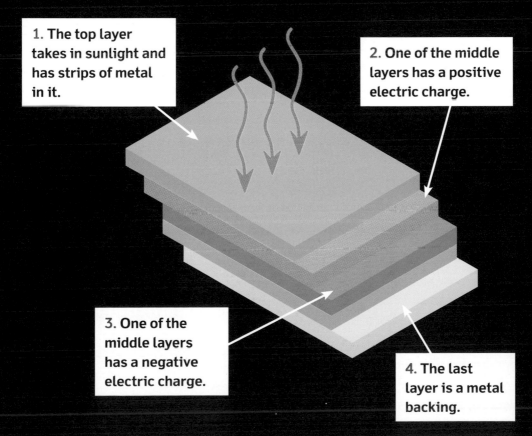

1. The top layer takes in sunlight and has strips of metal in it.

2. One of the middle layers has a positive electric charge.

3. One of the middle layers has a negative electric charge.

4. The last layer is a metal backing.

CSP use is growing around the world. In some countries, CSP plants are being set up as giant batteries. They collect heat during the day. Then they provide electricity at night.

PANELS AND POLLINATORS

Pollinators such as bees are animals that spread pollen around. They are necessary for plant growth. And people depend on them for growing crops. But these animals are losing their homes. Meanwhile, solar arrays take up land. Many arrays are set over gravel or grass. But that is changing. Minnesota has set a new standard. It encourages solar-farm owners to plant flowers that pollinators like. That way, solar farms become homes for pollinators. Other states are following Minnesota's example.

A solar heating system can warm the air in a room. It can also heat water that is used in sinks and showers.

Other solar technologies just make heat. For example, solar **thermal** technologies heat homes without electricity. They collect energy from the sun. They use it to heat water or air. The hot water or air flows to where people need it.

INTERNATIONAL SPACE STATION

The International Space Station (ISS) orbits approximately 240 miles (400 km) above Earth. Every 90 minutes, it completes a circle around the globe. The ISS has eight wings. It does not need them for flying. Instead, the wings are solar arrays.

Machines turn the arrays to face the sun. Extra power goes into batteries for when Earth blocks the light. The solar arrays produce enough electricity to power 40 houses. On the ISS, the arrays power six bedrooms and a gym. They also power several labs. Six astronauts live and work on the ISS. They run science experiments.

In 2021, some of the arrays were getting old. The oldest had been powering the ISS for more

The ISS was built over a period of 10 years.

than 20 years. They were starting to wear down. So, astronauts added new arrays next to the original ones. Together, the solar panels would power the ISS. They would make sure the ISS could continue its mission.

CHAPTER 4

SOLAR CHALLENGES

From 2009 to 2019, the price of solar power dropped 89 percent. Solar power became the cheapest of all energy options. This includes energy from fossil fuels.

Solar power is not perfect. The best solar cells can turn nearly 50 percent of the sun's energy into electricity. But this

The vast majority of solar energy worldwide comes from solar cells.

is only in the lab. As of 2021, most panels on the market harnessed 15 to 20 percent of solar energy.

So, scientists are designing more effective panels. One way is by using different materials. Most solar cells are made of silicon. This common element is found in rocks and sand. One promising new material is perovskite. Perovskites are tiny crystals made from several elements. The crystals can be printed with 3D printers. They can also be painted onto objects. Scientists are testing perovskite solar cells. Someday, these solar cells could perform better than silicon cells.

In 2020, perovskite solar cells in the lab could convert 25 percent of the sun's energy into electricity.

Another challenge is solar trash. Solar cells do not last forever. Panels can work for more than 25 years. But at some point, they become waste. The panels often contain toxic metals. In landfills, these metals could pollute surrounding areas. Some governments

require companies to recycle the panels.
But solar waste does not recycle easily.
And the process can be very costly.
So, scientists are designing solar cells
without toxic metals.

A third challenge has to do with energy
supply. People use electricity even when
the sun goes down. But solar panels only
produce power when the sun is shining.

To solve this problem, people can store
extra electricity in batteries. Storing
energy isn't cheap. The best batteries
use a soft metal called lithium. Lithium
batteries are expensive. They also
become less effective over time. So,
scientists are researching new materials

By 2020, the United States had enough solar energy to power nearly 18 million homes.

for batteries. As demand for battery storage increases, its costs will decrease.

Scientists are working to solve the challenges faced by solar power. And the world is responding. Solar power is the world's fastest-growing renewable energy source.